For A Moment

Kimberle Cavalieri

BookLeaf
Publishing

India | USA | UK

Presentation by *BookLeaf Publishing*

Web: www.bookleafpub.com

E-mail: info@bookleafpub.com

ISBN: 9789358367683

First edition 2023

I'd like to dedicate this book to all people who think they're not good enough. Please know you are more than good enough, and you are so worth it.

ACKNOWLEDGEMENT

I would like to thank my family and friends who support me unconditionally. You are the reason I can do things like this.

Not What You We're Thinking

As I get close to you and feel your warmth on my skin,
Your dark, decadent aroma invades my senses, lifting me.
And when I taste you, you fill not only my mouth but my blood, my cells, my soul
Taking me higher than ever, bringing me to new beginnings and awakenings.
I feel your warmth fill me from the inside out. A slow, deep burn.
But all too quickly you are gone. Leaving me wanting, lacking.
Until I have you again, then I'm reminded once more of what you do to me.
I will always come back for more coffee.

Too Quick

Where did the time go
I hope you remember me
My darling sweet child

Reminder

When I feel the light of the sun on my skin
I am reminded to let the light in
To fill my body, mind, and soul
And help me reach a new goal
To keep moving forward every day
And always keep the demons at bay
When I feel the light of the sun on my skin
I am reminded to let the light in
To disrupt the darkness of my mind
And to remind myself to be kind
To use the warmth and put on a smile
To keep walking that extra mile
When I feel the light of the sun on my skin
I am reminded to let the light in

Highs and Lows

Flying and soaring
The world falls away from me
Too soon it is over

It's over

The golden rays gifted from the sun,
warming the earth,
could never fill my heart with the amount of
warmth I feel, when you smile at me.
And because of this
The depths of vast, deep outer space could never
compare to the cold void of you being gone.
My world will never be the same.

Gone

I pick up the phone
I just want to hear your voice
But I'm all alone

Dark

The darkness that surrounds me
Is nothing
Compared to the darkness within me.
Vast, unending, crushing darkness.
Always making me feel
That I will never see another ray of light.
Blazing flames of light are beautiful,
but fleeting.
And all too soon
They are embers.
Once again,
I am left with darkness.

Light

How far have I come that the darkness within
me has shifted, moved, broken open by the
light? How far have I come that light, the
fleeting burst of blazing flames,
Which used to evade me,
Has encompassed me whole?
And now I squint with how much light I have.
How lucky am I to feel the warmth of light
inside me?
I know how far I've come and I will not go back
to the dark.
I am entirely too bright now.

For a minute

May I give you hugs
To let my soul speak to yours
To let me love you

Together

I stand before you
Ready to take on the world
With you I am free

Happiness

Four legs and a tail
Complete happiness abound
Life can't get better

A New Chance

Wipe away today
Wash away all the stress
Tomorrow begins

How stupid

To think I had you
And all that you did for me
I wasted my time

Soulmate

Together we make
A team no one can ever split
I am forever yours

Alone

You were there for me
And I squandered my time still
How selfish of me

Teacher

Take me away,
Hold my hand, and Lead me
To beliefs of worth
And don't forget
To teach me
I am enough

Darling

To see your wide smile
To hear your laughter so bright
My heart is now full

Workout

Rip and tear and pull
Every fiber does grow back
Stronger than before

Words

Slut loser loner
Words have no power over you
Unless you let them

Mind's Eye

Close your eyes and dream
Of another world far gone
And remember me

Mom

I have failed you, I
Have let you down more and more.
I know why you hate.